LIFE IN A LAKE

LIFE IN A LAKE

MELISSA STEWART

Lerner Publications Company
Minneapolis

This book could not have been completed without the assistance of Elise Ralph of the Large Lakes Observatory at the University of Minnesota, Duluth; Matt Julius of the Center for Great Lakes and Aquatic Sciences at the University of Michigan in Ann Arbor; Glen Warren of the Environmental Protection Agency in Chicago, Illinois; and Jeanette Morss of the Whitefish Point Bird Observatory in Paradise Point, Michigan.

Lerner Publications Company
A division of Lerner Publishing Group
241 First Avenue North
Minneapolis, MN 55401 U.S.A.

Website address: www.lernerbooks.com

Library of Congress Cataloging-in-Publication Data

Stewart, Melissa.
    Life in a lake / by Melissa Stewart.
        p.   cm. — (Ecosystems in action)
    Includes index.
    Summary: Describes how Lake Superior was formed and the interdependence of the plants and animals that live in and around it.
        ISBN: 0–8225–2138–5 (lib. bdg. : alk. paper)
    1. Lake ecology—Superior, Lake—Juvenile literature. 2. Superior, Lake—Juvenile literature. [1. Superior, Lake. 2. Lake ecology. 3. Ecology.] I. Title. II. Series.
QH104.5.S85 S74 2003
577.63'09774'9–dc21   2001008366

Manufactured in the United States of America
1 2 3 4 5 6 – JR – 08 07 06 05 04 03

CONTENTS

INTRODUCTION
WHAT IS AN ECOSYSTEM?

Every lake in the world is an ecosystem—a specific community of organisms and their nonliving physical environment. The nonliving elements in an ecosystem include the climate, the soil, the water, and the air. Lake Tahoe in Nevada and California is an ecosystem, and so are Lake Baikal in Siberia, Loch Ness in Scotland, and Lake Superior, which straddles the border between the United States and Canada. Each of these lake ecosystems is unique, with its own set of physical characteristics and inhabitants. Despite these differences, all the world's lakes have many things in common. That is why all lakes are grouped together as one of Earth's biomes.

Earth also has many other kinds of biomes. These include forests, deserts, grasslands, and wetlands. The Sonoran Desert in the Southwest is one ecosystem in the desert biome, while the Florida Everglades is an ecosystem in the wetlands biome. All the ecosystems in a biome have much more in common with one another than with ecosystems in other biomes. As a result, scientists are more likely to compare Lake Superior with Lake Tahoe or Lake Baikal than with the a tropical rain forest in Costa Rica or a cranberry bog in Massachusetts.

As in every other ecosystem on Earth, the organisms in Lake Superior need energy to grow and reproduce. The ultimate source of this energy is the sun. In most ecosystems, plants are the key primary producers. They make food for themselves by absorbing energy from sunlight and using it to power photosynthesis—a reaction in which carbon dioxide and water are converted into oxygen and glucose, a simple sugar. Some of the glucose is used to make starch, a substance that plants use to store energy. When primary consumers, such as snails, eat plants or other producers, the stored energy passes into their bodies.

In this way, energy from the sun moves up the food chain.

Very few plants can grow in Lake Superior's cold, choppy waters, so microscopic green algae, diatoms, and cyanobacteria form the base of this ecosystem's food chain. When a primary consumer grazes on green algae, it obtains the energy it needs to live and grow. In turn, secondary consumers, or predators, such as yellow perch, get their energy by preying on snails and other small creatures. When yellow perch die and sink to the bottom of the lake, their bodies provide food for decomposers—organisms that break down dead animals and plants and release nitrogen, phosphorus, and other nutrients that most living things need to survive.

In the last few decades, people have begun to realize that ecosystems are extremely complex. The delicate balance of interactions between organisms and their physical environment can be disrupted by human activities. If we are not careful, we can damage—or even destroy—our planet's precious ecosystems.

> ALL THE ECOSYSTEMS IN A BIOME HAVE MUCH MORE IN COMMON WITH ONE ANOTHER THAN WITH ECOSYSTEMS IN OTHER BIOMES.

ONTARIO

Nipigon River

N

NIPIGON

Kaministikwia River

KAMINISTIKWIA

THUNDER BAY

CANADA

UNITED STATES

PIGEON RIVER

Pigeon River

LAKE SUPERIOR

ISLE ROYALE

MINNESOTA

APOSTLE ISLANDS

COPPER HARBOR

KEWEENAW PENINSULA

WHITEFISH POINT

BAYFIELD

St. Marys River

DULUTH

ASHLAND

MARQUETTE

SAULT STE. MARIE

Soo Canals

MICHIGAN

PICTURED ROCKS NATIONAL LAKESHORE

St. Croix River

WISCONSIN

MICHIGAN

LAKE MICHIGAN

CHAPTER 1
A SUPERIOR LAKE

Lake Superior's jagged outline reminds some people of a wolf's head. If you look at a map you can picture Duluth, Minnesota, as the tip of the wolf's nose and Isle Royale as an eye. The animal's ears protrude into the Canadian wilderness, while its lower lip ends near Ashland, Wisconsin. The Keweenaw Peninsula helps define the wolf's lower jaw, and the northern boundaries of Michigan's Upper Peninsula—from Marquette to Sault Sainte Marie—form its thick neck. Every wolf belongs to a pack, and Lake Superior has four watery companions—Michigan, Huron, Ontario, and Erie.

Lake Superior is the largest freshwater lake in the world by surface area. It occupies 31,700 square miles (82,100 square kilometers)—as much as New Hampshire, Vermont, Connecticut, and Massachusetts combined. Lake Superior contains 3 quadrillion gallons (10 quadrillion liters) of water—10 percent of all the freshwater on our planet's surface. That's enough water to submerge all of North and South America under 1 foot (0.3 meter) of water.

In many ways, Lake Superior seems more like an ocean than a lake. If you stand along the lake's Michigan shoreline and

PICTURED ROCKS NATIONAL LAKESHORE, MICHIGAN

look out, all you see is water and waves. There is no sign of the Canadian coast more than 160 miles (260 kilometers) away. Duluth, Minnesota, the lake's westernmost port, is more than 350 miles (560 kilometers) from Sault Sainte Marie, where the lake's water drains into the St. Marys River, tumbles through a series of waterfalls, and then flows into Lake Huron.

Each year, about 2 feet (0.6 meter) of water flows into Lake Superior from rivers, streams, or underground sources, while 3 feet (0.9 meter) drains into the St. Marys River. But the overall water level isn't dropping because Lake Superior also receives 2.5 feet (0.76 meter) of water each year from rain and snow, and loses about 1.5 feet (0.46 meter) to evaporation. Thus, Lake Superior's annual inflow, outflow, precipitation, and evaporation are perfectly balanced. A closer look at the forces at work below the lake's surface show that they too play a role in maintaining the ecosystem's stability.

INSIDE LAKE SUPERIOR

Each winter, most of the world's lakes freeze over completely. While these lakes may

STORM WAVES CRASH ONTO LAKE SUPERIOR'S ROCKY SHORE.

seem dead to us, most do not freeze solid. Even though the water just below the ice is close to the freezing point, deep down it is warmer. This is where a variety of fish, frogs, turtles, and other creatures stay and wait for spring to return.

As a lake's icy covering melts, winds blow across the surface, stirring the water and its contents. Soon the upper layers of the lake have warmed, and the entire lake is about the same temperature. All summer long, the sun's rays shine down on the lake, further warming the water. Because warm water is less dense than cool water, the warm water tends to float on the top of the lake, while cooler water is concentrated below.

By midsummer, most lakes have stratified, forming three vertical layers. Sandwiched between a large upper layer of stable warmer water and a large lower layer of stable cooler water is the thermocline—a thin layer of water in which the temperature cools rapidly with depth. Because warm water cannot hold as much oxygen as cold water, the fish species and other organisms that require large quantities of oxygen move below the thermocline, while creatures that can survive with less oxygen remain above the thermocline.

In autumn, fewer hours of sunlight and strong breezes cause the warmer water at the top of the lake to cool quickly. When the surface water reaches 39° Fahrenheit (4° Celsius)—the temperature at which water is densest—it sinks rapidly, forcing up the water at the bottom of the lake. As in the early spring, the water throughout the lake "turns over," evening out the temperature and mixing oxygen and nutrients.

Things work a bit differently in Lake Superior. Although ice usually forms in the lake's shallow bays and inlets, it is rare for the entire lake to freeze over. All winter long, the lake continues to mix, as frigid winds whip across the open water in the middle of the lake. As a result, the entire lake stays cold all winter long. Frogs, turtles, and some other creatures that have no trouble overwintering in other lakes cannot survive in Lake Superior.

Like other large lakes, Lake Superior experiences two major turnover periods each year. The spring mixing usually begins in March and often continues into June. The shorter autumn turnover occurs in October or November. In the summer, the lake forms warmer and cooler layers, but those layers are broken up by a series of strong currents that flow along the lake's shores. In midsummer, the Keweenaw Current—the most significant near-shore current—acts like a narrow, racing river as it slices through the lake's quieter waters. In the process, it creates a vertical band of water called a thermal bar.

On the near-shore side of the thermal bar, sunlight penetrates to the bottom of the lake, causing the water to warm very quickly. The water on the far side of the thermal bar remains cooler. When water within the thermal bar reaches 39° Fahrenheit (4° Celsius), it sinks quickly and mixes a small area of the lake. As the column of surface water is sucked toward the lake's depths, it carries gases and an assortment of tiny creatures with it. At the same time, water and small animals from the bottom of the lake move up. This rich column of water attracts a variety of hungry birds from above and a handful of predatory fishes from below.

Lake Superior also experiences another unusual physical phenomenon—tidelike surges called seiches. Occasionally, strong winds or sudden changes in air pressure cause large quantities of water to pile up at one side of the lake. For the next few days, water throughout the lake rocks back and forth from one shore to another, like water in a frying pan that has been tipped and then laid flat. In the process, nutrients suspended in the lake's nepheloid layer—a region of cloudy, particle-rich water that is located just above the lake floor—are lifted to the sunlit surface. Seiches can temporarily alter lake water levels by as little as 3 inches (8 centimeters) or as much as 3 feet (0.9 meter).

LIFE IN THE LAKE

With an average annual temperature of just 40° Fahrenheit (4° Celsius) and a summertime peak of about 55° Fahrenheit (13° Celsius), Lake Superior is the coldest of the five Great Lakes. The lake's chilly waters cool the air above and surrounding

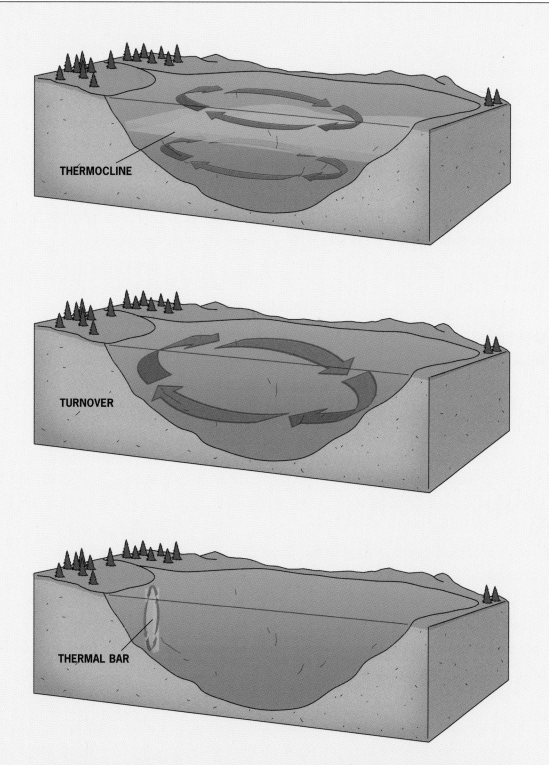

THERMOCLINE

TURNOVER

THERMAL BAR

LAKE SUPERIOR'S WATER SUPPLY IS CONTINUALLY MIXED BY SEASONAL WATER FLOW PATTERNS.

it, helping to keep nearby land comfortable on summer's hottest days. And because water temperatures tend to fluctuate more slowly than air temperatures, much of the lakeshore also experiences milder winter weather than nearby inland areas.

Depending on the weather conditions and the time of year, Lake Superior's waters range from towering, gray-green waves to bouncing, sapphire blue wavelets. Yet, most of the time, the water remains so crystal clear that it is possible to see objects more than 30 feet (9 meters) below the surface.

Superior's clear, frigid waters and sandy bottom are telltale signs of what scientists call a coldwater lake. Since most lake inhabitants are cold blooded, they are not able to control their body temperature. Whether a cold-blooded creature sits in the sun or hides in the shade, its body temperature matches the temperature of its surroundings. When its environment is chilly, a cold-blooded organism must conduct its life in slow motion. It moves and grows more slowly than it would if it lived in a warmer place. This explains why the average size of fishes and invertebrates (creatures without backbones) in Lake Superior tends to be smaller than the average size of cold-blooded creatures in other lakes.

Another less obvious characteristic of a coldwater lake is a lack of nutrients. Very few plants can survive in Lake Superior's cold, choppy waters and nearly sterile sediment. Without these important primary producers, populations of invertebrates, fishes, and other consumers are also relatively

> **SUPERIOR'S CLEAR, FRIGID WATERS AND SANDY BOTTOM ARE TELLTALE SIGNS OF WHAT SCIENTISTS CALL A COLDWATER LAKE.**

small. Still, many creatures call Lake Superior home.

Crayfish, snails, minnows, smallmouth bass, and a variety of insects are usually found very close to shore. As permanent residents of the lake's littoral zone, they do not venture into the open surface waters of the limnetic zone or the deep, dark regions of the profundal zone. But many other creatures do. The open waters are a good place for tiny zooplankton to find even smaller prey, while high above, hungry bald eagles search for large fish. Still other organisms are most often found in the lake's profundal zone—the deep dark waters that the sun's rays cannot reach. Here fish called burbot build mazes of tunnels in the bottom sediment and spend their days hunting for mysis shrimp or tiny amphipods called Diporeia.

Many fish move back and forth between the lake's zones. As lake herring and walleyes search for prey, they regularly cruise both the littoral and limnetic zones. Many other fish species are usually found in the lake's open waters, but migrate to shallow water or into the lake's tributaries when it is time to spawn, or lay their eggs. Several species of predatory fish spend their summers in the lake's limnetic zone, but retreat to the deep waters of the profundal zone for the winter.

A TALE OF LAVA AND ICE

Lake Superior's 1,826-mile (2,939-kilometer) shoreline includes dozens of large bays, inlets, and peninsulas. The arched northern lakeshore, which lies almost entirely within Canada's borders, features bold, rocky cliffs—some rising 100

SMALLMOUTH BASS (MICROPTERUS DOLOMIEUI)

WALLEYE (STIZOSTEDION VITREUM)

feet (30 meters) above the water's surface—and large, rugged tracts of forest. In many spots, rushing rivers drop rapidly from the interior highlands, creating rapids and dramatic waterfalls.

The lake's U.S. shoreline forms the northeastern border of Minnesota, touches the northernmost tip of Wisconsin, and meanders along Michigan's Upper Peninsula. The twenty-two Apostle Islands lie off the Bayfield Peninsula—a thumb of land that juts into the lake from the north coast of Wisconsin. To the east is the larger Keweenaw Peninsula and Michigan's

Pictured Rocks National Lakeshore, which boasts lovely, multicolored sandstone cliffs up to 300 feet (90 meters) high.

Near the center of the lake is Isle Royale—a 210-square-mile (540-square-kilometer) expanse of wilderness inhabited by beavers and birches, moose and maples, spruce and squirrels.

Lake Superior and the surrounding land have not always looked as they do today. Forces deep within our planet constantly reshape the land and oceans.

One billion years ago, all of Earth's land was part of a single supercontinent.

CHAPEL CREEK RUSHES INTO LAKE SUPERIOR.

As time passed, the area of land that now forms the American Midwest began to crack open and pull apart. The tear, or rift, began near Detroit, Michigan, and extended north through Lake Michigan and Lake Superior into northern Minnesota. There it abruptly changed direction, extending south until it ended in Oklahoma.

The rift was so deep that it passed all the way through Earth's solid crust into the mantle—a layer that contains hot, soft rock called magma. Like oatmeal, magma is very thick, but it can flow. For the next twenty-two million years, magma seeped through the rift and flowed onto the land as lava. When the molten material came into contact with air, it cooled to form a hard, dense rock called basalt. As the crust continued to pull apart, a broad, shallow basalt plain slowly formed in the Lake Superior area.

Ancient rivers flowed across some areas of the plain, depositing their loads of sand and mud. In other areas, shallow seas flooded the plain, and marine sediment slowly built up. As more time passed, the sediment compacted to form layers of different kinds of sedimentary rock. By five million years ago, the water had receded, and the land changed very little until the Pleistocene epoch—a period of time also known as the Ice Ages.

Between 1.7 million and 12,000 years ago, great changes in temperature affected the entire planet. In the very cold periods, rivers of ice called glaciers spread out over large areas of land and then retreated in warmer periods. This happened at least four times. Each time the glaciers expanded, the thick sheets of ice scraped the earth,

A MOOSE CALF (*ALCES ALCES*), ISLE ROYALE, MICHIGAN

flattening mountains, pushing boulders, and carving out craters. These glaciers scooped up most of the Lake Superior plain and compacted the land around it.

The rocky debris from the Lake Superior plain was deposited to the south and east—in New York, Ohio, Illinois, and Indiana. While few traces remain of the great rift that once divided the Midwest, the lake's shoreline still provides some evidence of the region's past. Most of the Canadian shore, the Keweenaw Peninsula, and Isle Royale are made of basalt—the hardened remains of ancient lava flows.

The Apostle Islands are carved out of sedimentary rock deposited long ago by freshwater rivers, and the sandstone cliffs of Pictured Rocks National Lakeshore formed from sediment deposited by ancient seas.

About eleven thousand years ago, as the last ice age glaciers melted, water filled the Lake Superior depression and a large area of surrounding land to form Glacial Lake Duluth. As time passed, geological forces deep within our planet caused much of the submerged land to rise. Water slowly drained from the rising land and flowed

GLACIERS HELPED CARVE THE BASIN THAT WOULD BECOME LAKE SUPERIOR.

APOSTLE ISLANDS, WISCONSIN

southward through Wisconsin's Brule River Valley to the St. Croix River. The water level of the ancient lake dropped more than 500 feet (150 meters) before incoming water from rivers such as the Nipigon, Kaministikwia, St. Louis, and Pigeon balanced the outflow.

The rivers, streams, and brooks brought more than just water to the lake. They also carried tons of sediment and a variety of living things. Over time, the organisms adapted to their new environment, and the Lake Superior ecosystem was born.

Thousands of other lakes formed around the same time as Lake Superior. Many of them still dot the northern regions of the world, but many others are long gone. Some evaporated as the planet's temperature rose. Others filled up with layers of sediment and decaying matter, leaving a bog or swamp in their place. Even though Lake Superior is now more than 1,300 feet (400 meters) deep in some places, eventually it too will disappear from Earth's surface. But for as long as it remains, Lake Superior will continue to be an important and unique ecosystem.

MULTICOLORED SEDIMENTARY CLIFFS ALONG PICTURED ROCKS NATIONAL LAKESHORE, MICHIGAN

CHAPTER 2
CLOSE TO SHORE

Even though Lake Superior is the largest lake in the world by surface area, it has a relatively small littoral zone. Glacial ice carved out the Lake Superior plain the way a scoop removes ice cream from its container. In most places, the bottom of the lake drops off quickly, so there are few areas with shallow water.

Most of Lake Superior's littoral waters lie within bays and harbors. Since sunlight can penetrate to the bottom of these shallow areas, the water here is often quite a bit warmer than water in other parts of the lake. The warmth and light make this a perfect environment for primary producers, such as algae and pennate diatoms.

Algae and diatoms belong to a large, diverse group of organisms called protists. Scientists believe that plants, animals, and fungi evolved from primitive protists millions of years ago.

Green algae form large, complex colonies of cells that live and work together. These colonies, which grow and spread along the surfaces of submerged rocks and logs, resemble slimy, miniature forests.

PENNATE DIATOMS *(PENNALES)* MAGNIFIED TWO HUNDRED TIMES

Pennate diatoms rest on solid surfaces or float in the water. Although some diatoms are circular or triangular, the pennate diatoms in Lake Superior's littoral zone are long and thin or boat shaped. Like green algae, pennate diatoms often cluster together and form colonies. All diatoms are protected by a hard, two-part shell. Like the top and bottom of a gift box, one half of a diatom's shell fits neatly inside the other half.

Some protists eat other organisms, but algae and diatoms make their own food. They contain chlorophyll and other pigments that capture energy from the sun and use it to power photosynthesis. Because Lake Superior has very few plants, protist producers are among the most important organisms at the bottom of the ecosystem's food chain. They are eaten by a wide variety of littoral zone inhabitants, including snails, mussels, clams, crayfish, and insect larvae.

BECAUSE LAKE SUPERIOR HAS VERY FEW PLANTS, PROTIST PRODUCERS ARE AMONG THE MOST IMPORTANT ORGANISMS AT THE BASE OF THE ECOSYSTEM'S FOOD CHAIN.

Snails glide along rocks and other solid surfaces, leaving behind a trail of gooey mucus. They spend most of their time scraping up green algae with their rasping tongues. Meanwhile, freshwater mussels and clams suck water into their bodies, filter out a variety of tiny organisms, and then expel the strained water. Most of the time, these shellfish rest in the bottom sediment with their shells open. But if they feel threatened, mussels and clams snap their shells shut and wait for the trouble to pass.

Despite their hard exteriors, shellfish are among the favorite foods of herring gulls, ring-billed gulls, raccoons, and muskrats. Raccoons and muskrats can crack the shells with their strong teeth, while gulls drop shellfish onto stony surfaces again and again until they finally break open. To avoid these predators, a mussel or clam may use its strong muscular foot to burrow into the sand.

INSECTS IN THE LAKE

Many insects spend their early lives in Lake Superior's shallow waters. Like snails and crayfish, the larvae of some mayflies suck up green algae all day long. Other young insects are decomposers that feed on detritus—tiny bits of decomposing matter and waste products that have fallen to the bottom of the lake. The larvae of midges and caddisflies spend most of their time crawling through sediment in search of these tasty morsels.

Caddisflies, midges, and mayflies leave the water when they grow up. As adults, these insects spend most of their time flying through the air in search of food or mates. But many other insects spend their entire lives in the lake.

The bodies of giant water bugs and predacious diving beetles are well adapted to their aquatic lifestyle. When a giant water bug is underwater, it uses its snorkel-like tail to breathe. It is a fierce predator that can easily subdue other insects and small fish. This bug grabs prey with its large folding front legs, pierces the victim with its strong, sharp beak, and then sucks out all the juices, leaving behind only a dried-up carcass. As the carcass slowly decays, it serves as food for other creatures. After two giant water bugs mate, the female wraps her legs around the male, spreads glue all over his back, and lays more than one hundred eggs there. The eggs will be safe from most predators until they hatch.

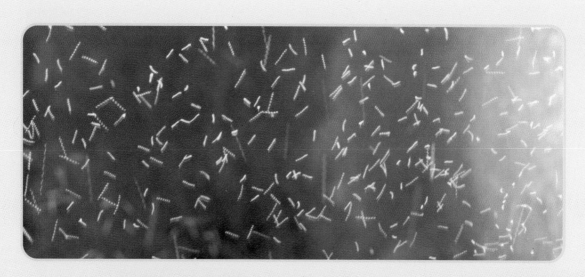

MIDGES (CHIRONOMIDAE) BREED AND HATCH IN THE SHALLOW WATER ALONG LAKE SUPERIOR'S SHORES BEFORE TAKING TO THE AIR AS ADULTS.

DEADLY DRAGONFLIES

One of Lake Superior's most ferocious predators might surprise you. It's the dragonfly nymph. Adult dragonflies usually live along the shores of open waterways. They are agile fliers and skilled hunters, preying on a variety of insects and other small creatures. After two adults mate, the female lays dozens of eggs in the water. A few days later, the nymphs begin to hatch.

While most larvae, such as caterpillars and grubs, look very different from the adults they become through metamorphosis, nymphs often look much like miniature versions of their parents. As nymphs grow, they molt, or shed their hard outer covering, several times, but they do not undergo the same kind of transformation as butterflies and beetles.

When dragonfly nymphs hatch, they are very hungry. They immediately start stalking for food in their watery surroundings. When a nymph spots a potential meal, it unfurls the long lower lip folded below its mouth and grabs the prey. Then the nymph devours the little animal with its strong jaws. Nymphs can easily attack the larvae of other insects, but they can also subdue adult insects and snails. Once in a while, a nymph may even manage to overpower a small fish, such as a fathead minnow, a longnose dace, or an emerald shiner.

While many young insects take just a few weeks to mature, a dragonfly nymph stays in the water for up to three years. During this time, it breathes through gills in its abdomen. When the nymph finally climbs out of the water, it grabs onto a hard surface and waits patiently for its hard exoskeleton to split open. When the dragonfly emerges, it is a winged adult with breathing holes instead of gills. After resting for a few minutes so its wings can dry, the insect zooms into the air and starts hunting for prey.

Predacious diving beetles spend a lot of time below the water's surface, so they need to take along plenty of air. Before each dive, the beetle stores a bubble of air under each wing. Like giant water bugs, predacious diving beetles are excellent swimmers and prey on other insects and minnows. In turn, they serve as food for waterfowl, crayfish, and a variety of fishes.

FISHES IN THE LITTORAL ZONE

A fish's streamlined body is well suited for moving through the water. A fish uses its paired pectoral and pelvic fins to start, stop, and turn quickly. The dorsal and anal fins help a fish keep its balance and stay still. A fish's tail, or caudal fin, waves from side to side, propelling the animal through the water.

Even though fish spend most of their time swimming and have the ability to cruise from place to place, most don't travel far. Quite a few fishes spend most of their lives in Lake Superior's relatively warm littoral waters. These include most members of the minnow family, smallmouth bass, brook trout, lake whitefish, pike, yellow perch, and lake sturgeon.

Minnows are a large group of very small fishes with long bodies. Smallmouth bass are larger, but like minnows, they spend all their time in the lake's shallow bays and do most of their feeding in the early morning and late afternoon. Smallmouths have golden brown or greenish backs and cream-colored bellies. They may grow up to 20 inches (50 centimeters) long and weigh as much as 5 pounds (2 kilograms).

Smallmouth bass spawn in the spring. Males build circular nests by fanning away debris with their fins. When a female arrives at a nest, she lays up to ten thousand eggs. Then the male releases sperm to fertilize the eggs. Females leave the nest, but males stay for a few days, to guard the eggs until they hatch. The young fish eat a variety of small organisms until they can handle the same foods as their parents—crayfish, insects, and smaller fish. Even as adults, smallmouth bass must always be on the lookout for predatory fishes, such as brook trout.

(TOP LEFT) **BROOK TROUT**
(SALVELINUS FONTINALIS)

(TOP RIGHT) **YELLOW PERCH**
(PERCA FLAVESCENS)

(LEFT) **LAKE STURGEON**
(ACIPENSER FULVESCENS)

(BOTTOM) **NORTHERN PIKE**
(ESOX LUCIUS)

Full-grown brook trout are about 16 inches (41 centimeters) long and weigh about 3 pounds (1 kilogram). These fish usually spend most of their lives in streams, but come to Lake Superior in search of food. In autumn, brook trout return to the tributaries where they hatched to create a new generation of fish. When a female finds the perfect spot for a nest, she uses her tail to scrape out a hole on the gravelly stream bottom. Then she deposits her eggs, and a male fertilizes them. The newly hatched trout fingerlings feed on everything from mayfly larvae to minnows, and, in turn, are eaten by turtles, otters, and birds such as mergansers, loons, and kingfishers. When the fingerlings are large enough, they swim to the lake, where they feed on smaller fish and an assortment of tiny aquatic organisms.

The lake whitefish is one of the most important species in Lake Superior. It has a small, toothless mouth and eats a variety of small organisms. These fish may weigh as much as 42 pounds (19 kilograms), but most adults are about 24 inches (61 centimeters) long and weigh close to 4 pounds (2 kilograms).

Pike and yellow perch spend most of their time swimming near the surface, but can also be found lurking near rocky drop-offs or along sandbars. The northern pike and muskellunge (muskie) belong to the pike family. Both have long, narrow bodies covered with small scales, a pointed snout, and a mouth full of formidable teeth. In Lake Superior, the northern pike usually grows to be about 3 feet (0.9 meter) long and may weigh as much as 8 pounds (4 kilograms). The muskellunge can reach 5 feet (1.5 meters) in length and weigh more than 70 pounds (30 kilograms).

In Lake Superior, pike are solitary, stealthy hunters that prey on smaller fish. Occasionally, they may also catch a duckling or a young muskrat. These fish do not make nests, and the males do not spend any time guarding the eggs. In spring, adults move to very shallow areas to spawn. As females scatter their eggs, males release their sperm. A few weeks later, a new generation of pike enters the world.

A yellow perch is short and round. It has a golden body with dark vertical bars on its sides. During the day, these fish often form large schools and swim in waters up to 30 feet (9 meters) deep, but at dawn and dusk, they move to the shallowest areas of the littoral zone and feed. Their favorite foods include smaller fish, insect larvae, snails, and a variety of other small creatures.

Yellow perch spawn in the spring. The females deposit long ribbons of eggs in shallow water, and males fertilize them. Many fish become inactive during the cold winter months, but perch continue to swim and feed all year long.

The lake sturgeon is a large, prehistoric-looking fish. It has a long, narrow body with several rows of bony plates and a snout that is rounded on top and flattened below. In most environments, lake sturgeon are no more than 6 feet (2 meters) long, but in Lake Superior they can live more than one hundred years, growing up to 8 feet (2.4 meters) in length and weighing more than 300 pounds (140 kilograms).

As a sturgeon cruises along the bottom of the littoral zone, four feelers hanging below its head help the fish locate food. When it senses prey, the giant fish slowly vacuums the lake bed, sucking an assortment of insects, snails, and other small creatures into its toothless mouth.

WATERFOWL AND SHOREBIRDS

Because plants, nutrients, and calm, warm waters are all in short supply, Lake Superior supports relatively few species of breeding birds. Only the hardiest waterfowl and shorebirds can survive here.

In early spring, mallards return to the lake from their winter homes in the southern United States and waste no time starting their families. Females lay nine to thirteen eggs in nests close to shore. About one month later, the eggs hatch, and the ducklings soon join their mother in the water. To feed, mallards tip themselves over and strain insects, protists, and other small organisms out of the water. These ducks often sleep on the water, where they are safe from bobcats, coyotes, and other large land predators.

Red-breasted mergansers are also a common sight in the coastal waters of Lake Superior. These ducks have a long, narrow, serrated bill that is perfect for grabbing and holding fish. Mergansers do not feed on the surface like mallards. Instead, they dive deep for larger prey.

Like mallards, most mergansers spend the winter in the southern United States and return to Lake Superior in early spring. The females build nests out of grasses and moss and line them with soft down feathers. Just a few hours after they hatch, the young are able to swim and hunt on their own.

While mergansers and other ducks hide their nests in secluded spots, gulls and common terns raise their young out in the open. After returning from their warm winter homes, large numbers of raucous females build loosely constructed, messy nests side by side on some of the lake's islands. If a hungry predator approaches a crowded colony, shrill cries of alarm quickly alert the entire community—usually confounding the hunter's efforts.

Gulls are large, long-winged shorebirds that fly with ease as they search for food. An adult herring gull has a gray back and black-tipped wings. Its head and tail are pure white. A ring-billed gull looks very similar,

but has a prominent black ring around its yellow bill. The feathers of younger gulls are much darker and more mottled.

Each spring when they return to Lake Superior, gulls look for new partners. When a male and female meet, they stretch their bodies upright, face one another, turn away, and then face each other again. A few minutes later, the male regurgitates some food and offers it to the female. If she is satisfied, the birds mate, and the female lays two to four eggs. Both parents feed the chicks until they learn to scavenge worms and other small creatures

RED-BREASTED MERGANSER (MERGUS SERRATOR)

along the lakeshore. After about five weeks, the youngsters are strong enough to fly and catch their own prey.

Common terns are abundant along some parts of the Lake Superior coastline. This smaller cousin of the gulls can be recognized by its white body, gray wings, black head cap, bright orange bill, and deeply forked tail. Common terns spend many hours each day flying above the lake in search of fish. When a hungry tern spots a potential meal, it plunges toward its target and may even dive a few feet underwater to catch the prey.

In the late spring and early summer, common terns build nests and search for mates. After the female lays two to five spotted eggs, the parents take turns sitting on them until they hatch about four weeks later. The chicks are covered with a thin covering of soft down feathers and greedily devour the small fish both parents bring to the nest. After about one month, the chicks learn how to fly and can begin to hunt for themselves. The following year, they will begin families of their own.

Other shorebirds, including the killdeer, the spotted sandpiper, and the

KILLDEER (CHARADRIUS VOCIFERUS)

Great Lakes piping plover, spend their summers feeding on invertebrates along the lake's shores. These small birds have many enemies, so they build nests that blend well with their surroundings. If a female and her chicks stay perfectly still, they are almost impossible to detect.

JUST PASSING THROUGH

While only a few kinds of birds raise families along Lake Superior's shores, many others spend some time at the lake during their annual migrations. Because Lake Superior is so large, it is a formidable barrier for birds trying to fly due north or south. Each spring, many birds follow the shores of Lake Huron and Lake Michigan on their journey north. But when they reach Lake Superior, they must make a decision. Should they try to fly directly over the lake—knowing there is no place to stop for a rest or a meal—or should they follow the lake's shoreline east or west and go around the lake?

Many birds choose the longer, safer route around the lake's perimeter. Others go to the Keweenaw Peninsula

and spend a few days resting and eating before they take off across the lake. Then they stop over at Isle Royale before finishing their journey. Still others fly to Whitefish Point and cross at the lake's narrowest part.

As a result of this migratory behavior, Hawk Ridge near Duluth, Minnesota, is a great place to see hawks in the autumn, while Whitefish Point, Michigan, is a better place to watch for owls and a variety of songbirds. Each year, hundreds of thousands of common loons spend several weeks at the lake during their autumn migration. Double-crested cormorants also spend an extended period on the lake. While they are there, these skilled hunters fill up on fish and a variety of small invertebrates, including crayfish.

Although migratory birds spend only a few hours or a few days at the lake, they still contribute to the ecosystem. As primary and secondary consumers, they help control prey populations. And their waste matter adds precious nutrients to the ecosystem.

MAMMALS ALONG SUPERIOR'S SHORES

Small birds make a tasty meal for the weasels and mink that live in wooded areas along the shores of Lake Superior. While weasels usually hunt on land, mink are excellent swimmers and feed on fish and shellfish as well as rabbits, mice, shrews, birds, and muskrats. The mink has a slender, arched body with a long neck, short legs, and a bushy tail. Its thick coat of reddish brown fur is interrupted by a white throat patch. At night, the mink sleeps in a den or burrow close to the edge of the lake. During the day, it hunts for prey.

While mink are fast asleep, raccoons are busy catching fish and probing the lake's shallow waters for shellfish, snails, and other treats. Using their nimble paws, raccoons can also steal birds' eggs or pick and eat berries, seeds, and nuts.

A raccoon is about the size of a large house cat and has bushy, grayish brown fur, a ringed tail, a pointed snout, and a black mask across its eyes. During the day, this clever animal rests in tree hollows. Each spring, adult females give birth to as many as seven young. Mothers nurse the kits for

(LEFT) **MUSKRAT (*ONDATRA ZIBETHICUS*) AND** (RIGHT) **MINK (*MUSTELA VISON*)**

seven to nine weeks. Then the youngsters must start to forage on their own.

Mice and rats can be found in just about every environment on Earth, but their larger relatives the beaver and the muskrat live only in watery environments. Beavers are common in the ponds, streams, and wetlands that border Lake Superior, but they are rarely seen in and around the lake itself. These large rodents feed primarily on water plants, which are in short supply in Lake Superior.

Muskrats, however, do come to the lake in search of food. They have a more varied diet that includes shellfish, snails, and crayfish. These mammals have reddish brown fur, a light gray belly, a wide tail that is thick in the middle but flat on the sides, partially webbed back feet, and yellow teeth. Muskrats sleep through the winter in lodges made of grasses and mud. During the summer, an adult couple works together to raise several litters of youngsters.

The mammals that contribute to the Lake Superior ecosystem may be skilled swimmers, but they never journey far from shore. They have no reason to, because the creatures they prey on are easy to find in the littoral zone. Shellfish, crayfish, snails, waterfowl, shorebirds, and an array of tiny organisms also spend their whole lives in the lake's shallow waters. It is where they find food and mates, raise their young, and eventually die. This does not mean, however, that the rest of the lake is devoid of life. Lake Superior's open surface waters support a completely different community of living things.

RACCOONS (PROCYON LOTOR)

CHAPTER 3
OPEN SURFACE WATERS

No well-defined line separates Lake Superior's shallow littoral zone from the wide-open surface waters that make up the limnetic zone. Nevertheless, as the lake deepens, the dominant forms of life gradually change. Populations of green algae and pennate diatoms slowly give way to different kinds of primary producers. Millions of tiny cyanobacteria float near the water's surface, photosynthesizing from sunrise to sunset. All around them centric diatoms do the same. Like their pennate relatives, these diatoms are protected by a two-part shell. But instead of being long and thin, centric diatoms radiate out from a central point. They resemble pinwheels, bicycle wheels, and eight-sided stars. These diatoms are excellent

sources of nutrients, providing large quantities of energy to an assortment of microscopic animals called zooplankton.

In most of the world's lakes, rivers, seas, and oceans, zooplankton are the chief primary consumers of algae, diatoms, cyanobacteria, and other microscopic photosynthesizers. In Lake Superior's limnetic zone, tiny copepods, water fleas, and other zooplankton rise to the surface

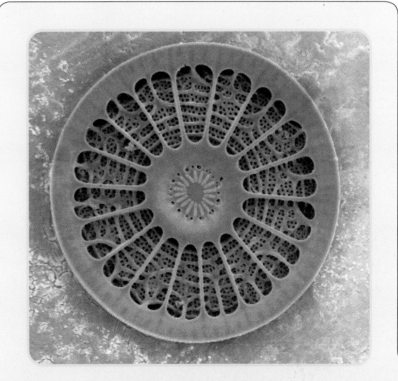

CENTRIC DIATOM (CENTRALES)

each evening and gorge themselves all night long. When daylight returns and their enemies awaken, the tiny animals migrate to the safety of deeper waters.

Water fleas, such as daphnia, swim with jerky, zigzag motions and look like pregnant canaries with long, feathery antennae. Each one has a transparent body, making it possible to see its beating heart and the food in its gut.

Copepods, such as cyclops, have prominent eyespots, long antennae that move like miniature oars, and two long tails. Two large egg sacs often hang below the bodies of females. While some copepods are nearly transparent, others are milky white or grayish brown. Although they are voracious feeders that suck tiny prey into their bodies, copepods also serve as food for a variety of fish species.

IN MOST LAKES, WALLEYES LIVE IN THE DEEPEST, DARKEST WATERS, BUT LAKE SUPERIOR IS SO COLD AND DEEP THAT WALLEYES FEEL MORE AT HOME IN THE LIMNETIC AND LITTORAL ZONES.

PART-TIME RESIDENTS

While most inhabitants of Lake Superior spend their entire lives in one zone, some of the lake's fishes are more cosmopolitan. The lake herring is one of the fishes that cruise the waters of the littoral and limnetic zones. They spend most of their time swimming in schools, eating tiny organisms and avoiding enemies.

In most lakes, walleyes live in the deepest, darkest waters, but Lake Superior is so cold and deep that walleyes feel more at home in the limnetic and littoral zones. These predators can grow up to 30 inches (80 centimeters) long and weigh as much as 10 pounds (5 kilograms). Walleyes are named for their unusual pearly eyes, which have a reflective layer of pigment that helps them see to feed in murky waters or at

WE OWE IT ALL TO CYANOBACTERIA

The plants, animals, and other organisms we see around us today have not always been here. Originally, our world was a fiery, inhospitable place. Even after the planet cooled, the atmosphere was laden with carbon dioxide and a variety of poisonous chemicals. A few primitive organisms managed to survive the harsh conditions and reproduce on early Earth. They probably lived deep underground or at the bottom of the ocean.

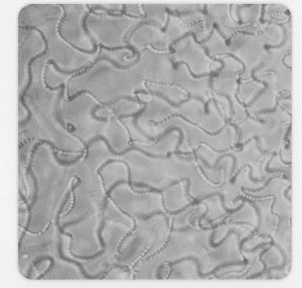

Many scientists believe that our planet and its life evolved together. The earliest fossil evidence of life is close to 4 billion years old. As these ancient organisms slowly evolved, some eventually moved to the top of the ocean. After even more time passed, some developed the ability to conduct photosynthesis. Among these early photosynthesizers were the cyanobacteria. Scientists believe that the first cyanobacteria lived on Earth about 2.5 billion years ago.

As cyanobacteria absorbed the sun's rays and manufactured their own food, they released oxygen. Over hundreds of millions of years, these tiny organisms pumped out enough oxygen to completely saturate the world's oceans. Oxygen had nowhere to go but up into the atmosphere. As millennia passed, the amount of oxygen in the atmosphere continued to increase. Today oxygen is the second most common component of the atmosphere.

When the sun's ultraviolet (UV) rays struck oxygen molecules (O_2) that had risen into the upper atmosphere, some split into oxygen atoms (O) and combined with other oxygen molecules to form ozone (O_3). Over time, a thick ozone layer shrouded the planet, shielding the newly evolved organisms below it from some of the harmful UV rays.

Like all animals, humans need to inhale oxygen to live. And our delicate bodies would burn to a crisp without the protective ozone layer. If it weren't for cyanobacteria, humans never would have evolved.

dawn and dusk, when little light is available. Walleyes dine on zooplankton as well as on smaller fish.

In early spring, female walleyes lay their eggs in shallow areas of the lake. Then males arrive and release sperm in the same general area. Neither parent guards the eggs or cares for the fry, or young fish. Young walleyes are on their own. They spend their days hunting for tiny creatures and avoiding their many enemies.

While lake herring and walleyes move from zone to zone on a daily basis, lean lake trout make seasonal migrations. They spend their summers in the lake's limnetic waters but migrate to the profundal zone for the winter. These torpedo-shaped fish may grow up to 4 feet (more than 1 meter) long and weigh more than 40 pounds (20 kilograms).

Like most fish, lake herring, walleyes, and lean lake trout are dark on the top and sides, but have a light-colored belly. This coloring, called countershading, is the perfect kind of camouflage for creatures that live in open waters. When a larger predatory fish looks up from below, the camouflaged fish's light undersides blend

(LEFT) **FRESHWATER COPEPODS** *(COPEPODA)*

(BELOW) **LEAN LAKE TROUT** *(SALVELINUS NAMAYCUSH)*

with sunlight streaming down from above. And when a hungry raptor, such as a bald eagle or an osprey, looks down from above, the fish's upper body blends with the dark water surrounding it.

THE ULTIMATE PREDATORS

In the Lake Superior ecosystem, bald eagles and osprey are the top predators. These ferocious hunters spend their days scanning the lake's open surface waters for fish. Both birds have many features that help them catch prey.

Using their large, keen eyes, eagles have no trouble spotting the telltale flash of fish scales. The clawlike talons on their feet are perfect for stabbing and grasping their targets. Strong leg muscles help the birds carry slippery victims back to shore. Sharp, curved beaks and strong jaws allow eagles to tear and chew flesh quickly and efficiently.

Eagles are also masters of flight. Because their long, wide wings catch breezes and columns of warm air rising from the ground, they can soar through the sky without exerting much energy.

They usually spot fish from the air, dive down, and snatch the prey out of the water. If the catch is very heavy, the eagle may swim to shore by rowing with its wings. When fish are in short supply, bald eagles may hunt small mammals and other birds. They also scavenge for carrion.

Bald eagles usually mate for life. Each couple works together to build a large stick nest at the top of a tree or along a lakeside cliff and then raises a new family there every year. Each female lays one to three white eggs in March and incubates them until they hatch. During this period, the male brings food to his mate.

After the eggs hatch, both parents guard the nest and catch food for the young. Because food is often in short supply, many eaglets do not survive to adulthood. A young eagle usually makes its first flight when it is about three months old, but its parents continue to provide some care for several more months.

Most of the bald eagles along Lake Superior's shores stay there all year long, but ospreys do not. They hunt and nest at the lake during the summer, but fly south in the winter. Ospreys are smaller than eagles, but they are also expert fishers. As an osprey flies, it scans the water with its sharp eyes. When it notices the iridescent flash of a fish's scales, the bird dives steeply—sometimes plunging its talons 3 feet (1 meter) below the surface to seize its target.

Osprey build huge, basketlike nests between jagged rocks or in high tree branches on the lake's forested shores. Couples return to the same nest each spring. The female usually lays three or four eggs and incubates them until they hatch about one month later. Both parents feed and care for the young birds until they learn to hunt for themselves. Then the ospreys begin life on their own.

Most of the time, juvenile and adult raptors feed on trout, pike, and yellow perch. But these large fishes are not the lake's only big inhabitants. Another community of big fishes spends all its time in the lake's deepest, coldest waters.

OSPREY (PANDION HALIAETUS)

CHAPTER 4
DEEP, DARK WATERS

In Lake Superior, the limnetic zone extends downward about 115 feet (35.1 meters). Below that is the profundal zone. In these frigid waters, life is less abundant and less diverse, and it proceeds at a slower pace. Because sunlight cannot reach the profundal zone, no primary producers live here. These waters are home to a few small invertebrates and a few species of fish.

One of the most interesting profundal animals is the hydra—a primitive relative of corals, sea jellies, and sea anemones. In Lake Superior, large numbers of hydra cling to rocks as deep as 1,300 feet

BECAUSE SUNLIGHT CANNOT REACH THE PROFUNDAL ZONE, NO PRIMARY PRODUCERS LIVE HERE. THESE WATERS ARE HOME TO A FEW SMALL INVERTEBRATES AND A FEW SPECIES OF FISH.

(400 meters) below the water's wavy surface. When hydra are resting, they look like gooey red blobs. But at feeding time, each one unfolds its body to reveal a half-dozen fingerlike tentacles. These tentacles may look graceful as they sway through the water, but they are actually deadly weapons. Each one is lined with dozens of nematocysts— tiny barbed harpoons full of poison that can subdue prey in minutes. Once the target is immobilized, the hydra pulls the helpless creature into its mouth and begins the slow process of digestion.

Most of the time, hydra dine on Diporeia and mysis shimp—tiny organisms that drift through the water like snowflakes. Diporeia belong to a group of tiny invertebrates called amphipods. These tannish gray creatures have long antennae and seven pairs of legs. They are most active at night and swim on their sides.

Mysis shrimp are larger than Diporeia, but smaller than the shrimp we eat. Each evening, they swim to the lake's surface waters to feed on smaller zooplankton until the sun rises. Then swarms of shrimp return to their deepwater home. In some areas of the lake, mysis shrimp migrate more than 950 feet (290 meters) each day. Like the zooplankton in the lake's limnetic zone, mysis shrimp feed at night to avoid predators. Nevertheless, these tiny animals are an important food source for profundal-zone fishes.

DEEP-LAKE FISHES

Shortjaw ciscoes, kiyis, and bloater chubs are all members of the cisco family—close relatives of trout. While these small, silvery fishes are residents of the lake's profundal zone, they usually live no more than 600 feet (200 meters) below the surface. They feed primarily on Diporeia and mysis shrimp.

All ciscoes rely heavily on their lateral lines—specialized sensory systems that extend along the sides of most fishes. As water presses against a fish's lateral lines, nerve impulses help the animal sense its position and rate of movement. Lateral lines also allow ciscoes to detect rocks and other inanimate objects by sensing vibrations as water is reflected off them.

A HYDRA (HYDRA) CAPTURES ITS PREY BY STINGING IT WITH POISONOUS TENTACLES.

FISH FOOD OF CHOICE

Mysis shrimp are not true shrimp, but they are distantly related. Scientists believe that, like the saltwater shimp we eat, the ancestors of mysis shrimp inhabited the ocean. But as Ice Age glaciers spread over Earth's surface, ocean water and the life it contained was pushed southward. When the ice receded, some seawater became trapped in glacial depressions and mixed with the melted ice that formed lakes. Because primitive mysis shrimp were hardy creatures, they managed to survive and gradually adapted to their new freshwater home.

Most scientists classify mysis shrimp as zooplankton, but they are significantly larger than most other zooplankton and have a longer lifespan. Most zooplankton live only a few days or a few weeks, but mysis shrimp often live two years. The adults mate under the ice in winter, and females carry the developing youngsters in a pouch until late spring or early summer.

The size of mysis shrimp makes them the prey of choice for many fish species. And because they are an excellent source of protein and fat, fish that consistently feed on mysis shrimp grow more quickly than fish that feed on the other kinds of zooplankton.

Deepwater sculpins are bizarre fish with wide, flat heads and short, tapered bodies. Instead of scales, these small, grayish brown creatures have a prickly covering and prominent cheekbone spines. Other kinds of sculpins live in salt water. Scientists believe that—like the ancestors of modern mysis shrimp—deepwater sculpins originally lived in arctic waters, but were pushed southward in front of advancing glaciers. When the ice sheets retreated, the fish remained in Lake Superior and other deep, cold lakes formed by glaciers.

Deepwater sculpins never leave the lake's profundal waters. They spawn year-round, laying eggs in shallow, open depressions that they dig in the sandy lake-bed sediment with their stiff pectoral fins. Sculpins spend most of their days tunneling through the sediment in search of Diporeia and mysis shrimp. In turn, these fish serve as food for siscowet, burbot, and other predatory fishes.

Siscowet, the deepwater cousins of lean lake trout, grow up to 4 feet (over 1 meter) long and weigh as much as 50 pounds (20 kilograms). They have stout bodies and small heads. Cruising the lake at depths of

A DEEPWATER SCULPIN *(MYOXOCEPHALUS THOMPSONI)* IN THE GREAT LAKES AQUARIUM, DULUTH

300 feet (90 meters) and deeper, siscowet normally hunt ciscoes, sculpins, and other profundal dwellers. Occasionally, they leave the profundal zone and hunt closer to the surface. Like sculpins, siscowet mate and spawn in the deepest parts of the lake. They are slow-growing fish that do not reach maturity until they are at least six years old and may live to be more than thirty-five years old.

The smaller burbot spends most of its time in the profundal zone, but in midwinter it moves to the littoral zone or swims into tributaries to spawn at night under the ice. Females lay eggs in sandy or gravelly areas, and then males release their sperm. While the eggs mature, the long, cylindrical adults return to their deepwater home, where they feed on sculpins and other fishes. Burbot have developed a special system for catching prey. They dig long trenches in the sandy sediment on the bottom of the lake and wait at one end. Unaware of the trap, smaller fish swim along the trenches—right into a hungry burbot's mouth.

Like organisms in the littoral and limnetic zones, burbot, sculpins, mysis shrimp, Diporeia, and other profundal dwellers make important contributions to the Lake Superior ecosystem. Whether they are producers, consumers, or decomposers, all lake inhabitants help keep the ecosystem in balance.

BURBOT *(LOTA LOTA)* LIVE IN THE ICY DEPTHS OF LAKE SUPERIOR.

CHAPTER 5
MAINTAINING THE BALANCE

Although Lake Superior is a complex and dynamic environment, it is more vulnerable than many other ecosystems. An ecosystem's ability to tolerate crises and eventually recover is directly related to its biodiversity—how many different species it supports. Unfortunately, Lake Superior's ability to bounce back is threatened by its relative lack of biodiversity. As a result, when even one of the lake's physical conditions is altered or when just one population of organisms is harmed, the results may be felt throughout the entire ecosystem.

In most lakes, plants are the major primary producers, while algae, diatoms, and cyanobacteria are less important. In these environments, a disease that ravages the diatom population, for example, would not lead to a major calamity. But Lake Superior is different. It has few plants and only a handful of microscopic species that act as primary producers. As a result, the entire ecosystem is extremely dependent on diatoms. If large numbers of Lake Superior's diatoms suddenly died off, the ecosystem would have a great deal of trouble rebounding. Without enough food, many small invertebrates and other primary consumers would starve. Then, it would be only a matter of time

> **ALTHOUGH LAKE SUPERIOR IS A COMPLEX AND DYNAMIC ENVIRONMENT, IT IS MORE VULNERABLE THAN MANY OTHER ECOSYSTEMS.**

before secondary consumers felt the impact too.

Primary producers are not the only organisms that have difficulty surviving in Lake Superior. A variety of amphibians and reptiles inhabit the littoral zone of most lakes, but cold waters and long winters make it nearly impossible for these animals to live in Lake Superior. The lake's midges and mayflies endure the coldest months by overwintering as eggs. Caddisfly larvae and dragonfly nymphs can freeze solid in winter and thaw out in spring. But many small invertebrates are not so hardy. They cannot grow and reproduce in Lake Superior. Dozens of waterfowl and shorebird species inhabit most North American lakes, but only a few species nest and raise young along Lake Superior's shores. With fewer organisms in each niche, the Lake Superior ecosystem is less able to cope with sudden changes and to react to environmental challenges.

MOVING AND MIXING

While many of Lake Superior's inhabitants spend their entire lives in a single zone,

A DRAGONFLY (ANISOPTERA) NYMPH

THE DISGUISED DECOMPOSER

While wriggling, wormlike midge larvae are easy prey for a variety of hungry predators, caddisfly larvae are more difficult to spot. Using bits of decaying leaves, pebbles, and anything else they can find, caddisfly larvae build tubelike cases around themselves. When a hungry fish gets too close, caddisfly larvae retreat into their protective cases and stay perfectly still until the danger has passed. Then they continue to graze on the thin layer of decaying organic material at the bottom of Lake Superior.

As a caddisfly larva moves along the lake bed, it drags its case along. Several small hooks on the animal's tail grip the tube tightly as the insect scrambles from place to place. Like a hermit crab, the larva needs to change homes as it grows. However, while a hermit crab is content to live inside the old shells of other animals, a caddisfly larva builds all its own cases.

After a few months of feeding, caddisfly larvae are ready to transform into land-dwelling adults. During the pupal stage, when they are changing into adult caddisflies, their gills are replaced by breathing holes, and wings emerge. Now the caddisfly is a small, drab, mothlike insect with long, slender antennae. Caddisflies are poor fliers, and most do not eat during their short adult lives. During the day, they hide in the shade. At night, they congregate in large numbers and search for mates.

Some females drop masses or strings of eggs into the water, while others lay each egg individually on the water's surface. The eggs sink to the bottom of the lake, and within a few hours, new larvae have hatched, and the adults have died.

others do not. Lake herring and walleyes move between the littoral and limnetic zones on a daily basis. Other species spend their summers feeding in the lake's open surface waters, but winter in the profundal zone. At mating time, many fish species move into the lake's fast-flowing tributaries. Diporeia and mysis shrimp spend their days in the lake's deepest waters, but migrate to the surface each night to feed. A variety of young insects are perfectly at home in the lake's shallow waters, but as adults they live on land.

These animal movements—along with periodic and seasonal changes in the lake's temperature—help disperse and recycle the lake's limited nutrient supply. When birds, fish, and other organisms die or produce waste materials, gravity carries the material downward. In the littoral zone, a variety of small creatures, including the larvae of caddisflies and midges, feed on and break down detritus. In the profundal zone, bacteria are the primary decomposers. A large portion of the nutrients these creatures release becomes suspended in the lake's nepheloid layer.

During the lake's twice-yearly turnovers and occasional seiches, the nutrients as well as energy and oxygen are redistributed throughout the lake. In addition, the lake's unique thermal bar and the currents it creates cause localized mixing and create a productive feeding ground for a variety of lake residents. In these ways, the living and nonliving components of the lake work together to maintain the ecosystem's balance.

By now you know that a wide variety of organisms play important roles in the Lake Superior ecosystem. But did you know that people influence the ecosystem, too? In fact, our actions have a tremendous impact on the health and vitality of the lake. As you will soon see, sometimes we do things that help the lake ecosystem, but sometimes we harm it.

CHAPTER 6
PEOPLE AFFECT LAKE SUPERIOR

Nearly four hundred years ago, French explorer Étienne Brulé became the first European to lay eyes upon the largest lake in North America. He named it Lac Supérieur, meaning "Upper Lake." But Brulé was certainly not the first person to view Superior's raw beauty. Several Native American societies had been thriving along the lakeshore for thousands of years. They knew the lake as Gitchee Gumee, meaning the "shining big sea water."

The Ojibwe, Cree, and Dakota peoples fished in the lake's waters and hunted in its coastal forests. While they freely took whatever they needed to survive, the Native Americans were also careful not to waste anything.

When Pierre Radisson and Médard Chouart des Groseilliers first tested the waters of Lake Superior in 1659, they were impressed by the area's stark splendor as well as with the lake's abundance of delicious whitefish and 400-pound (200-kilogram) lake sturgeon. At the time, the lake was home to some 150 fish species. Each one played an important role in an intricate food web that had gradually developed over ten thousand years.

A few years later, Daniel Greysolon, Sieur Dulhut—for whom Duluth, Minnesota, is named—explored much of the area

PIERRE RADISSON WAS AMONG THE FIRST EUROPEAN EXPLORERS TO WITNESS THE BEAUTY OF LAKE SUPERIOR.

between Thunder Bay and the Mississippi River. Along the way, he made alliances with Native American groups and opened up safe routes for French fur traders.

Beaver hats were all the rage in Europe, and beavers were becoming increasingly scarce in areas to the east. The price of pelts was well worth the trouble of exploring unknown territory. By the early 1700s, a network of fur-trading posts had been set up throughout the region, and Grand Portage, Minnesota, became a major trading center.

By the 1830s, most of the beaver, mink, and other fur-bearing mammals in the forests surrounding Lake Superior had been killed, and the European fur fad began to wane. But just as the fur industry petered out, the logging and fishing industries started to gain momentum.

EXPLOITING THE LAND

When European explorers surveyed Lake Superior's shores, they encountered thick forests of pine, fir, spruce, cedar, birch, and aspen. At the time, the area was too remote to make logging worthwhile. But by the 1800s, eastern woodlands had been exhausted. The logging industry looked to the Lake Superior region as the next great source of lumber.

Throngs of loggers moved into the area. For a while, the north woods of Michigan, then Wisconsin, and finally Minnesota were the world's greatest producers of forest products. By 1900, though, most of the woodlands near the lake had been depleted. Loggers packed their belongings

LOGGERS IN MICHIGAN, 1895

and headed out to the Pacific Coast. The Lake Superior logging boom ended as quickly as it had begun.

Today logging is once again big business on Lake Superior's north shore. By selectively cutting existing forest stands, loggers are able to supply pulp and paper mills near Thunder Bay and Duluth with the raw materials they need without destroying native woodland ecosystems. But that does not mean the industry isn't harming the lake.

A dangerous chemical called dioxin is the unavoidable by-product of using chlorine to bleach paper pulp. In animal studies, dioxin has been shown to upset normal sexual and nervous system development. It may also impair behavior and learning.

Although papermakers have made great strides in reducing their dioxin emissions, as a group they still cannot meet the U.S. Environmental Protection Agency's dioxin guidelines. They have, however, had greater success in other areas. Since 1973 they have reduced their discharges of oxygen-depleting materials by as much as 70 percent. Still, the paper industry must continue its efforts to further reduce pollutant emissions.

> BY THE MID-1800S, COMMERCIAL FISHING HAD BECOME A MAJOR SOURCE OF REVENUE IN THE AREA. YEAR AFTER YEAR, LAKE SUPERIOR'S TOTAL ANNUAL CATCH EXCEEDED 100 MILLION POUNDS (50 MILLION KILOGRAMS).

EXPLOITING THE WATER

According to British trader Alexander Henry, in the mid-1700s, "a skillful fisherman could take five hundred [whitefish from the lake] in two hours." By the mid-1800s, commercial fishing had become a major source of revenue in the area. Year after year, Lake Superior's total annual catch exceeded 100 million pounds (50 million kilograms).

The whitefish population began to dwindle in the 1890s, so commercial fishers turned to lake trout. By 1920 lake trout were nearly gone, and the fishing industry was relying most heavily on lake herring. Lake Superior's most desirable species were being picked off one by one, and the entire ecosystem was beginning to suffer. Fish populations could not reproduce quickly enough to replace the huge quantities being caught by humans. Meanwhile, the populations of invertebrates and zooplankton normally eaten by fishes were dramatically increasing.

Around 1930 the annual catch of fish dropped below 8 million pounds (4 million kilograms). In the 1950s, most of the lake's large, predatory fish were nearly wiped out.

MORE BOUNTY FROM THE LAND

Much of the land along Superior's southern shores was once richly endowed with deposits of iron, copper, and other useful minerals. In the 1840s, American settlers began vast mining projects to remove these materials.

Tons of copper excavated from mines dotting the Keweenaw Peninsula were loaded onto boats in Copper Harbor,

BOXES OF FISH ARE READY TO BE SHIPPED FROM THE HARRY GOLDISH LAKE SUPERIOR FISH COMPANY, 1920.

Michigan, and transported eastward. It has been said that Michigan's rich supply of copper helped secure the North's victory in the Civil War (1861–1865). By the 1880s, iron exports from upper Michigan and Lake Superior's Minnesota shores had outstripped earlier copper yields.

By 1900 Lake Superior's mines produced 75 percent of America's iron ore, excavating close to 8 million tons (7 million metric tons) each year. Like big-time logging enterprises, mining companies laid down mile after mile of railroad track and built the most impressive shipping vessels the world had ever seen. In 1910 iron ore comprised approximately 50 percent of all bulk cargoes shipped on the Great Lakes. The iron was taken to processing plants in and around Pittsburgh, Pennsylvania, where it was smelted to make steel. On the return trip, trains and freighters carried coal.

World War I (1914–1918) and World War II (1939–1945) created enormous demands for steel. During the war years, Lake Superior's mines provided as much as 40 million tons (36 million metric tons) of iron per year. When supplies of the iron-containing minerals hematite and magnetite began to decline in the 1950s, steel-industry scientists quickly developed efficient methods for extracting iron from taconite and other minerals. By 1970 Minnesota mines were producing 54 million tons (49 metric tons) of taconite annually. Experts are confident that the remaining supply of taconite will satisfy the needs of the American steel industry for many generations to come.

Like other natural resources, Lake Superior's minerals come at a price. In the 1950s, Duluth resident Alden Lind noticed

WORKERS WASHED TAILINGS (RESIDUE) FROM COPPER PRODUCTION INTO LAKE SUPERIOR.

"billowing pea-green clouds" in Lake Superior's normally crystal-clear waters. Lind soon realized that the clouds only appeared down current of a large mining company. He suspected the company was dumping something hazardous into the lake. Although company executives ignored Lind's questions, local citizens did not. They formed the Save Lake Superior Association and, eventually, forced the company to stop dumping its taconite tailings—finely ground particles that contain asbestos-like fibers—into the lake.

Processing iron ore also results in other harmful waste products. These include carbon monoxide, sulfur dioxide, and mercury. Carbon monoxide is a greenhouse gas that contributes to global warming. Warmer temperatures in recent years have made it possible for zebra mussels to reproduce in some parts of Lake Superior. They have also disrupted the normal pattern of turnovers and decreased the lake's winter ice cover, which has increased evaporation from the lake. Scientists do not yet know how all these changes have affected the ecosystem.

Sulfur dioxide reacts with gases in the atmosphere to form acid precipitation. When the acidic rain or snow falls into the lake, it can kill snails and worms. It can also damage the nervous systems and weaken the bones of vertebrates. In some cases, the acid may react with rocks on the lake bed and release aluminum, which can damage the gills of fish.

AN EXCAVATOR DIGS FOR TACONITE IN 1954.

Mercury can also harm a variety of organisms. Like so many other chemicals, it accumulates in body tissues and is passed up the food chain. Scientists have identified top-level fishes, such as lean lake trout or walleye, with mercury levels one million times higher than the water they swim in.

When people eat those fish, the mercury gradually builds up in their bodies too. Eventually, adults may suffer from memory loss and the inability to concentrate, as well as trembling and slurred speech. Children may experience developmental delays, and babies born to women who have eaten large amounts of mercury may have a number of birth defects. To protect people from these serious health problems, many local and state health departments have developed guidelines that let people know how much fish is safe to eat.

THE GROWTH OF TRANSPORTATION

The shipping enterprises and railroad systems developed to support the mining industry were soon being used for a variety of purposes. Although the area surrounding Lake Superior is not suitable for agriculture, Duluth-Superior Harbor has ranked as the United States's largest grain shipment port since the 1880s. Even more grain is shipped out of Thunder Bay, Canada.

The grain that passes through the Duluth-Superior Harbor grows in western Minnesota, North and South Dakota, and Montana. It is transported to the port cities by railroad, temporarily stored in grain elevators, and then shipped east through the Great Lakes and the St. Lawrence River system.

In recent years, many farms in the upper Midwest have begun to grow significant quantities of sugar beets, potatoes, soybeans, flax, corn, oats, and barley. These crops are also exported through Lake Superior's harbors.

The Soo Canals at Sault Sainte Marie, completed in 1855, brought a brand-new industry to Lake Superior. Passenger steamboats began carrying tourists to the lake. Many visitors were interested in the gorgeous scenery, while others came primarily to hunt, fish, and "tent" along the lake's untamed shores. In the early 1900s,

Great Lakes cruise ships carried up to eighty thousand passengers a year to Lake Superior.

Not long after that, a new form of transportation, the automobile, began to draw business away from cruise ships. But the popularity of motorcars did not diminish the lake's popularity as a vacation spot. Soon, many people drove to and stayed at small resorts and lakeside cabins.

FROM CABINS TO CONDOS

The small resorts and cabins remained popular vacation spots for many decades, but in the 1990s, tourists-turned-retirees, baby boomers with money to spare, and urban refugees began to fuel a new wave of growth and development along some Superior shores. Cabins with clotheslines are quickly being replaced by condo clusters with golf courses.

Some parts of the Superior lakeshore are already threatened by failing septic systems. Because the region's soils simply cannot absorb the added wastewater, it flows along bedrock and empties into the lake. But the most obvious solution—installing municipal sewer lines—would increase pressures to further develop the area, which would cause additional soil erosion.

Both vacationers and residents are drawn to the shores of Lake Superior because they value clean air, peace and quiet, and safe and friendly communities— all within easy reach of North America's largest and cleanest freshwater lake and vast areas of publicly owned woodlands. The problem is that if too many people want to live near Lake Superior, the area's natural beauty will eventually be lost as bulldozers make way for housing developments,

parking lots, and shopping malls to accommodate all the newcomers.

THE THREAT OF EXOTIC SPECIES

Beginning in the late 1800s, humans have accidentally or deliberately added a variety of exotic species to the lake. The first invader was the brown trout—a European species brought to North America by settlers and stocked in Wisconsin waters. It didn't take long for the hardy species to spread throughout the Great Lakes.

A few years later, rainbow trout—locally known as the steelhead—entered the Lake Superior ecosystem. These West Coast natives quickly adapted to their new surroundings, becoming one of the lake's most common limnetic species. After peaking in the 1960s, steelhead populations suddenly declined. Overharvesting by commercial fishers had taken their toll. After many years of careful monitoring, the lake's steelhead are now beginning to make a comeback.

Rainbow smelt were introduced into Michigan lakes in the early 1900s and

A TOUR BOAT PASSES THE CLIFFS ALONG LAKE SUPERIOR'S SHORE. MORE DEVELOPMENT ALONG THE SHORE COULD THREATEN THE DELICATE LAKE SUPERIOR ECOSYSTEM.

appeared in Lake Superior around 1930. These foot-long, colorful fish are sensitive to bright light and warm waters. During the day, they spend most of their time swimming in schools in cooler, deeper areas of the lake's littoral zone. At night they rise to the surface to feed on a variety of small organisms.

To survive in the lake's open waters, two more recent invaders—three-spine and four-spine sticklebacks—take advantage of some special defense mechanisms. Each of these fish has hard, protective plates instead of scales and a line of sharp spines running along its back. Even though these features help sticklebacks survive attacks by larger fish, they have become an important source of food for the lake's predators.

By the 1960s, four species of salmon had also learned to survive in Lake Superior. The small population of Atlantic salmon, and larger populations of chinook, coho, and pink salmon, were added to the lake to satisfy the fishers who spend their weekends and vacations on the lake. Chinook, coho, and pink salmon are native to the Pacific Northwest. They have long bodies covered with small, rounded scales, and move into tributaries to spawn. As adults, they feed on

EXOTIC SPECIES, SUCH AS THE THREE-SPINED STICKLEBACK (GASTEROSTEUS ACULEATUS), COMPETE WITH NATIVE FISH POPULATIONS FOR FOOD AND NESTING SITES.

insects and smaller fishes, especially rainbow smelt and lake herring.

Over the years, scientists have carefully monitored how exotic species affect the lake's natural inhabitants. As a result, they know that rainbow smelt and sticklebacks compete with lake herring, and they suspect that some salmon species interfere with the spawning behavior of native trout species. They also know that, if left to their own devices, the sea lamprey—an invader that first entered Lake Superior in 1938—could quickly wipe out the lake's top predatory fishes, which would eventually disrupt the entire ecosystem.

Sea lamprey are normally ocean dwellers, but they can survive in freshwater if enough prey is available. Each spring, 20-inch-long (50-centimeter-long) eel-like adults swim into Lake Superior's tributaries to spawn. The adults soon die, but a few weeks later, the fertilized eggs hatch. The blind, toothless larvae burrow into the muddy bottom and remain there for several years, eating whatever tiny creatures they can strain out of the water. Finally, the young sea lamprey transform into predatory adults and swim to the lake.

The sea lamprey is an aggressive parasitic fish equipped with rows of sharp, inward-pointing teeth and a tongue like a carpenter's file. When attacking an unsuspecting fish, the sea lamprey approaches the side of its prey's body, clamps on with its circular suction-cup mouth, and rasps out a hole with its rough

THE SEA LAMPREY (PETROMYZON MARINUS) HAS SHARP TEETH IN A SUCTION-CUP MOUTH THAT CLAMPS ONTO THE SIDE OF ITS PREY.

tongue. A blood-thinning chemical in the sea lamprey's saliva keeps the wound open for hours or days—until the predator eats its fill or the victim dies. Each sea lamprey can destroy up to 40 pounds (20 kilograms) of salmon, lean lake trout, lake whitefish, burbot, and other large fishes during the twelve to eighteen months it spends in the lake.

In the 1950s, scientists began developing effective methods for controlling sea lamprey. These include barriers that prevent the parasites from reaching their breeding grounds and chemicals that kill sea lamprey larvae. These techniques have greatly reduced the number of sea lamprey in Lake Superior. Unfortunately, they have also affected the lake's small native populations of less aggressive parasitic and nonparasitic lamprey.

The impact of invasive sea lamprey on the Lake Superior ecosystem extends far beyond the devastation of a few fish species. As sea lamprey decimated the lake's top predators, bloater chubs and other lower-level fishes grew larger and became more abundant. This, in turn, affected the lake's populations of mysis shrimp and Diporeia, as well as the zooplankton they feed on. As the lake's natural food chain was disrupted, the entire biological community was knocked out of whack.

In the mid-1980s, the Eurasian ruffe slipped into Duluth-Superior Harbor as transoceanic vessels released ballast water into the lake. As large freighters unload their cargo, they fill tanks with water to help balance and stabilize the ship. When the vessels take on new cargo, they no longer need the water, so they discharge the ballast—and any freeloading aquatic creatures—into the local water. Scientists believe that as many as 30 percent of the invasive creatures in the Great Lakes entered in ballast water.

The Eurasian ruffe is a relative of the yellow perch and walleye. This small but aggressive fish feeds in the lake's littoral zone at night. To detect prey in the darkness, the ruffe relies on sensory hairs called neuromasts. Protective, bony fins discourage northern pike, muskies, and other bigger fishes from eating it. These special features help the ruffe dominate just about any ecosystem it enters. The ruffe grows fast, reproduces in great numbers, and can adapt to a wide variety of environments. This makes it a threat to yellow perch, walleyes, and other fish species, as well as the small organisms they feed on.

Eurasian ruffe are certainly not the only invaders to enter the Great Lakes through ballast water. Zebra mussels entered the Great Lakes in the 1980s and have spread at an alarming rate. These troublesome shellfish often attach themselves to and clog the interior surfaces of boat motors and the water intake pipes of power plants and water-treatment facilities. Large clumps also grow on top of native clams and mussels and suffocate them.

While zebra mussels have caused problems in the lower Great Lakes, Lake Superior's cold waters and lack of food and nutrients inhibited their growth and reproduction for many years. However, unusually warm weather in the late 1990s gave zebra mussels an opportunity to greatly expand their populations in some areas of the lake. Some scientists are concerned that zebra mussels will spread to other areas of Lake Superior if the warm weather continues.

The spiny waterflea was first spotted in Lake Superior in 1987. This European relative of the native daphnia has a milky white body with four pairs of legs; stout swimming antennae; a large, black eye; and a long, sharp, barbed tail spine. The spiny waterflea is a skilled hunter and reproduces quickly in the warm summer

THE ZEBRA MUSSEL *(DREISSENA POLYMORPHA)* IS ANOTHER EXOTIC SPECIES THREATENING THE GREAT LAKES ECOSYSTEM.

months. In addition, the little invader's toothpick-like tail discourages many potential predators.

Another recent Lake Superior invader is the round goby. This small, bottom-dwelling fish appeared in Duluth-Superior Harbor in 1995. Since then, it has reproduced rapidly, spawning up to six times each summer and laying as many as thirty thousand eggs a year. In its natural environment, the round goby eats shellfish and large invertebrates as well as fish eggs, small fish, and insect larvae. In Lake Superior, the goby displaces native fishes, eats their young, and takes over prime habitats. It is too early to tell what kind of long-term impact the round goby will have, but scientists are very concerned.

SAVING LAKE SUPERIOR

People living in the Lake Superior area are now working hard to address the problems associated with exotic species, overfishing, and land development, but other hazards are more difficult to control locally. The most significant of these is pollution. While mining companies and paper manufacturers have made great strides in limiting the pollutants they release into the lake, many of the pollutants that plague Lake Superior's waters drift there through the air. Some come from as far away as Central America. As a result of global wind currents, weather patterns, and local geography, toxins tend to migrate to the Great Lakes region and then remain there, where they can end up in the bodies of the wildlife.

Because Lake Superior has fewer nutrients, fewer microorganisms, and less sediment than the other Great Lakes, it is particularly vulnerable to hazardous chemicals. Once toxic materials enter the ecosystem, they tend to stay there, gradually accumulating in the tissues of birds, fish, and mammals.

In most lakes, pollutants sink to the bottom and are trapped in the sediment. But in Lake Superior, the small particles are often incorporated into the nepheloid layer. As seiches, currents, and biannual turnovers mix the lake waters, the particles in the nepheloid layer circulate through the lake. Like the lake's nutrients, the pollutants are recycled.

Polychlorinated biphenyls (PCBs) are a family of synthetic organic compounds that were once used in electrical and mechanical equipment. They were banned in the 1970s, when laboratory experiments showed that they can cause birth defects and cancer in animals, but they still can be found in the environment. Recent studies have shown that levels of PCBs are 33 million times higher in the bodies of Lake Superior's herring gulls than in the surrounding water.

In the 1970s, dichloro-diphenyl-trichloroethane (DDT), a harmful pesticide that is no longer used in most parts of the world, nearly decimated local populations of osprey and bald eagles. When female raptors absorbed DDT from their prey, they produced eggs with extremely fragile shells. In many cases, the eggs broke before the chicks hatched. The survival of these important predators is largely due to carefully monitored captive breeding programs and to the reintroduction of the captive-bred birds into the Lake Superior environment.

DDT and PCBs are not the only dangerous chemicals that have entered the Lake Superior ecosystem. Scientists now keep close tabs on nine key pollutants. This effort and many other programs designed to protect and preserve Lake Superior are the result of a long-term international commitment.

Since the 1970s, the U.S.–Canadian Great Lakes Water Quality Agreement, the U.S. Clean Water Act, and the Lake Superior Binational Program have been providing researchers with millions of dollars to study the lake and find ways to reduce the impact of hazardous materials entering the ecosystem. With all these programs in place, scientists hope that the lake will eventually be restored to its former glory.

When explorer and geologist Henry Rowe Schoolcraft first set eyes on the lake in 1820, he was overwhelmed by the incredible beauty of Lake Superior. He pulled out his journal and quickly jotted: "One cannot help fancying that he has gone to the ends of the earth and beyond the boundaries appointed for the residence of man." Perhaps, one day, Lake Superior will once again live up to Schoolcraft's passionate description.

COVE AT MINER'S CASTLE, PICTURED ROCKS NATIONAL LAKESHORE

WHAT YOU CAN DO

PROTECTING LAKE ECOSYSTEMS

One of the best ways to learn about Lake Superior is by visiting it. Many of the national lakeshores and parks along the borders of the lake have nature study programs and interpretive trails that teach people about the wildlife that lives there. By staying on the trails, you can enjoy your surroundings and know that you are causing no harm.

To protect Lake Superior and other lake ecosystems, we must make informed choices about the role we will play in their future use. What can you do to protect lakes and other waterways near your home? Here are some suggestions.

• If you fish, be careful not to spread exotic species from one body of water to another. Use separate gear in each body of water and do not catch small fish in one place and use them as bait in another spot. If you catch an alien invader, release it immediately into the same body of water. Take a shower and wash your clothes as soon as you get home, so no eggs will accidentally enter another waterway.

• Don't pour chemicals such as gasoline, paint, or household cleaners into sinks, bathtubs, toilets, or the ground. They may seep into a groundwater system and pollute it. When the poison comes into contact with fish and other aquatic creatures, it can kill them. Contact a local government agency to find out whether your town or city has a day designated for the safe collection and disposal of chemicals.

• Use safe alternatives to harsh household cleaners. Instead of commercial window cleaner, try a mixture of vinegar and water. Your windows will sparkle. A paste of baking soda and water effectively cleans sinks, tubs, and toilets.

• Don't throw trash and other garbage into a roadside ditch or any body of water. Not only is trash unsightly, it can make fish and other animals sick. Some communities have water clean-up days. You might want to participate in one. If you do, be sure to do so with an adult's supervision and remember to wear gloves and boots.

- Conserve water. It may not seem like much, but each time you get a drink and let the faucet run until the water gets cold, you are wasting water. Keep a water bottle in the refrigerator. You should also avoid letting the water run continuously while you are washing your hands and face or brushing your teeth, and you should take showers rather than baths. A typical bath requires twice as much water as most showers.
- Plant flowers, grasses, shrubs, and trees that are native to your area. They will need less water and soil to survive.
- Use wood chips or bricks on pathways, rather than concrete, so rain can seep into the ground. Less runoff means pesticides and fertilizers are less likely to find their way into lakes and other waterways.
- Collect rainwater in a barrel and use it to water plants. Keep the barrel tightly covered when it isn't raining to prevent mosquitoes from laying their eggs in it.
- Join a community organization that takes an active role in lake preservation and conservation.

WHAT HAPPENS IN THE FUTURE? YOU CAN BE INVOLVED

If you live in the Lake Superior area, you can contact the Great Lakes Alliance or other local organizations that are interested in preserving and protecting the lake. You can also read local newspapers and magazines to learn more about the lake. You can even write letters to the governor of your state or to your state senators and representatives. Your input can really make a difference!

To write to the senators from your state:

The Honorable (name of your senator)
United States Senate
Washington, D.C. 20510

To write to your representative in Congress:

The Honorable (name of your representative)
U.S. House of Representatives
Washington, D.C. 20515

WEBSITES TO VISIT FOR MORE INFORMATION

The following websites contain a wealth of information. All suggest further Web links for more information.

The Great Lakes Aquarium

<http://www.glaquarium.org>
Located in Duluth, Minnesota, this facility showcases seventy species of fish and other creatures found in Lake Superior and the other Great Lakes. At this website, you can learn about many of Lake Superior's inhabitants, find out why preserving freshwater ecosystems is so important, and get a close-up view of the lake's underwater world through a special webcam.

Lake Superior

<http://www.pca.state.mn.us/water/basins /superior/>
This site, which was developed and is maintained by the Minnesota Pollution Control Agency, features information about the lake and links to a variety of organizations that are studying and working to preserve it.

Large Lakes Observatory

<http://www.d.umn.edu/llo/>
This is the home page for an organization that does a great deal of research on Lake Superior. Check out this site to find out what the researchers are up to.

Minnesota Sea Grant

<http://www.seagrant.umn.edu/>
The University of Minnesota's Sea Grant Program oversees and provides funding to many scientists studying Lake Superior's physical characteristics and inhabitants. At this site, you can learn about ongoing research efforts or order a variety of publications that describe the natural history of the lake and the wildlife found there.

Whitefish Point Bird Observatory

<http://www.wpbo.org>
Located on Lake Superior's Michigan shoreline, this nature center provides information about the birds that live and breed in or near the lake. Scientists at the center also monitor annual bird migrations in the area.

FOR FURTHER READING

Ashworth, William. *The Late, Great Lakes: An Environmental History.* New York: Knopf, 1986.

Josephs, David. *Lakes, Ponds and Temporary Pools.* Danbury, CT: Franklin Watts, 2000.

Katz, Sharon. *The Great Lakes.* Tarrytown, NY: Benchmark Books, 1999.

McClung, Robert M. *Lost Wild America: The Story of Our Extinct and Vanishing Wildlife.* Hamden, CT: Linnet Books, 1993.

Orr, Richard. *Nature Cross-Sections.* New York: DK Publishing, Inc., 1995.

Patent, Dorothy Hinshaw. *Biodiversity.* New York: Clarion Books, 1996.

Sayre, April Pulley. *Lakes and Ponds.* New York: Twenty-First Century Books, 1996.

Scott, Michael. *Ecology.* New York: Oxford University Press, 1995.

VanCleave, Janice. *Ecology for Every Kid: Easy Activities that Make Learning about Science Fun.* New York: John Wiley & Sons, 1996.

Whitman, Sylvia. *This Land Is Your Land: The American Conservation Movement.* Minneapolis: Lerner Publications Company, 1994.

GLOSSARY

amphipod: a small invertebrate

ballast water: water that is taken in when cargo is unloaded or released when cargo is added to a ship. The weight of the water helps balance and stabilize the ship.

biodiversity: the variety of living things found in an ecosystem

biome: a kind of naturally existing community of living organisms. Forests, deserts, wetlands, and lakes are all biomes.

cold blooded: unable to maintain a constant body temperature

countershading: a kind of camouflage in which an aquatic creature is dark on top and light on the bottom to provide protection from enemies above and below

crust: Earth's outer layer

decomposer: an organism that breaks down the remains of dead plants and animals

detritus: tiny bits of decomposing materials

ecosystem: a specific community of living organisms, along with the place they live and the physical conditions that surround them. Lake Superior, Chesapeake Bay, and the Everglades are examples of ecosystems.

exotic species: an organism that has been transplanted to a new environment

food chain: a feeding order in which energy is passed from one living organism to another

glacier: a large, moving body of snow and ice

invertebrate: an animal that has no backbone

larva (pl. larvae): an early stage of development in the life of many kinds of animals. In insects, it refers to the young of species that undergo complete metamorphosis (egg, larva, pupa, adult).

lateral line: a sensory organ that runs horizontally along a fish's body

limnetic zone: the open surface waters of a lake

littoral zone: the shallow, coastal waters of a lake

magma: hot, molten rock that makes up Earth's mantle. When magma spills onto the surface, it is called lava.

mantle: the layer between Earth's crust and the outer core. It is made of molten rock called magma.

metamorphosis: the process by which some young animals transform into adults

molt: to shed or lose the exoskeleton, feathers, skin, or other kind of outer covering as an animal grows

nematocyst: one of the tiny barbed harpoons on the tentacles of a hydra

nepheloid layer: a layer of particle-rich water that is normally suspended just above the bottom of Lake Superior

neuromast: a hairlike sense organ located along the lateral lines of some fishes

nutrient: a substance, especially in food, that is needed for healthy growth

nymph: a young insect that develops through incomplete metamorphosis. Nymphs do not pass through a pupal stage before becoming adults.

photosynthesis: the process plants and certain other organisms use to change sunlight, carbon dioxide, and water into energy in the form of sugars and starches

primary consumer: an organism that eats primary producers

primary producer: an organism that carries out photosynthesis to make food for itself

profundal zone: the deep, dark waters of a lake

protist: a member of the group of simple living organisms that are not considered plants or animals

rift: a crack in Earth's crust

secondary consumer: an animal that eats primary consumers

sediment: small pieces of rock, soil, or plant debris

seiche: a tidelike surge caused by strong winds or sudden changes in barometric pressure. A seiche causes large quantities of water to pile up at one side of a lake.

spawn: to produce and release eggs and sperm; usually refers to the breeding activities of fish and other aquatic animals

thermal bar: a region of vertical mixing in a column of water that occurs when near-shore water warms more quickly than water in the middle of a lake

thermocline: the thin middle layer of water that develops between an upper layer of stable warmer water and a lower layer of stable cooler water when temperature differences cause a lake to stratify in the summer

zooplankton: small, often microscopic, animals that float in water

INDEX

ABOUT THE AUTHOR

Melissa Stewart has always been fascinated by the natural world and is a careful observer. Before becoming a full-time writer, she earned a bachelor's degree in biology from Union College and a master's degree in science and environmental journalism from New York University. She then spent a decade working as a science editor.

Ms. Stewart has written more than a dozen critically acclaimed children's books about animals, ecosystems, earth science, and space science. She has also contributed articles to a variety of magazines for adults and children, including *Science World, Odyssey, National Geographic World, Natural New England,* and *American Heritage of Invention and Technology.* She lives in Marlborough, Massachusetts.

PHOTO ACKNOWLEDGMENTS

The photographs in this book are reproduced with the permission of: © Layne Kennedy/CORBIS, pp. 2–3, 17; © TOM STACK & ASSOCIATES, pp. 9 (Terry Donnelly), 16 (Terry Donnelly), 19 (John Gerlach), 20 (Brian Parker), 25 top left (Tom & Therisa Stack), 25 middle (Tom Stack), 28 (Joe McDonald), 31 (Thomas Kitchin), 32 (Thomas Kitchin), 36 top (Ken W. Davis), 38 (Dave Watts), 63 (Terry Donnelly); © Richard Hamilton Smith/CORBIS, p. 10; ©State of Minnesota, Department of Natural Resources, pp. 15 (both), 25 (bottom), 41; © David Muench/CORBIS, p. 18 (left); National Park Service, p. 18 (right); © Peter Johnson/CORBIS, p. 22; © Science Pictures Limited/CORBIS, pp. 23, 35, 40, 45; USDA Photo, pp. 25 top right (Ken Hammond); © Perry J. Reynolds, p. 29; © Jim Zuckerman/CORBIS, p. 33; Great Lakes Aquarium, pp. 36 (bottom), 42, 43; © Papilio/CORBIS, p. 46; © Bettmann/CORBIS, p. 48; State Archives of Michigan, p. 49; Minnesota Historical Society, pp. 51, 53, 55; © North Wind Picture Archives, p. 52; © Phil Schermeister/CORBIS, p. 56; © Frank Lane Picture Agency/CORBIS, p. 57; © CORBIS, p. 58; © Dave Haas/Image Finders, p. 60 Maps and illustrations on pp. 8 and 13 by Tim Seeley. Bottom border by National Park Service. Cover photography by © Layne Kennedy/CORBIS.